The

P

by Geoff Patton
illustrated by David Clarke

RISING★STARS

the school

SCHOOL

to Sam's house

BOB'S CORN COBS

2

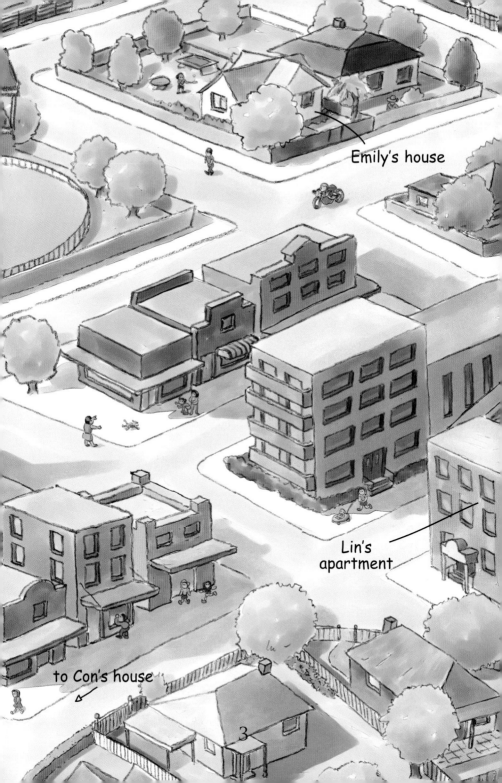

Emily's house

Lin's apartment

to Con's house

3

Hi. My name is Emily,
but you can call me the
rollerblade princess.

Dad

me
(Emily)

Chapter 1
Home on Wheels

I *love* to rollerblade. When I am in the house, I don't walk, I rollerblade.

I rollerblade in the kitchen.

I rollerblade in the bedroom.

I rollerblade in the bathroom.
The bathroom can be *very* tricky!
But it is *so* exciting.

I rollerblade until my dad says,
'Don't rollerblade in the house, Emily.'
'But I am the rollerblade princess,' I say.

Dad says, 'Princesses don't rollerblade.'
But I'm sure they do.

Chapter 2
Wheeling the Dog

I *love* to rollerblade. When I take
Puddle for a walk, I don't walk,
I rollerblade!

We rollerblade to the playground.

We rollerblade to the beach.

We rollerblade to the park.
The park can be *very* tricky!
But it is *so* exciting.

I rollerblade until Toola Oola says,
'Don't rollerblade in the park, Emily.'
'But I am the rollerblade princess,' I say.

Toola Oola says, 'Princesses don't
rollerblade.' But I'm sure they do.

Chapter 3
Shopping on Wheels

I *love* to rollerblade. When I go to
the supermarket, I don't walk,
I rollerblade!

I rollerblade to the milk.

I rollerblade to the bread.

I rollerblade to the apples.
The apples can be *very* tricky!
But it is *so* exciting.

I rollerblade until Ms Green says,
'Don't rollerblade in the
supermarket, Emily.'
'But I am the rollerblade princess,'
I say.

Ms Green says, 'Princesses don't
rollerblade.' But I'm sure they do!

Chapter 4
Meals on Wheels

I *love* to rollerblade. When we go
to the café, I don't walk, I rollerblade!

I rollerblade to the chips.

I rollerblade to the chicken.

I rollerblade to the drinks.
The drinks can be *very* tricky!
But it is *so* exciting.

I rollerblade until Molly says,
'Don't rollerblade in the café, Emily.'
'But I am the rollerblade princess,'
I say.

Molly says, 'Princesses don't
rollerblade.'
'Maybe princesses *don't* rollerblade,'
I think to myself.

Chapter 5
Princess on wheels

I *love* to rollerblade. But people
don't love me when I rollerblade!
I say, 'I'm giving up rollerblading.
I will watch TV instead.'

On TV there is a story about a
princess. The princess is taking her
dogs for a walk. She is wearing
rollerblades. 'I just *love* to rollerblade,'
says the princess.

'**Yes**!', I say.

'I knew princesses went rollerblading!' I shout.

21

Survival Tips

Tips for surviving rollerblading

1 If you are rollerblading in the bathroom always wear your swimsuit. You never know if you will end up in the bath.

2 If you are rollerblading and taking your dog for a walk, watch out for cats. If your dog decides to chase, it can get very messy!

3 When rollerblading in the supermarket, watch out for those trolleys. A head on crash is not a pretty sight.

4 Don't try meals-on-wheels unless you are really good. Meals-on-wheels can be fun, but meals-on-clothes-on-wheels is not.

5 Stay away from gardens. Rollerblades and flowers just don't mix.

Riddles and Jokes

Emily	What's grey with 8 wheels?
Molly	An elephant on rollerblades.
Emily	What's grey, has 8 wheels and is very dangerous?
Molly	An elephant rollerblading down a hill.
Emily	Who's faster than a speeding rocket and packs your bags at the checkout?
Toola Oola	That's easy it's Supermarket man!
Toola Oola	How long have you been rollerblading?
Emily	Since I was five years old.
Toola Oola	You must be really tired.